IGNEOUS

Lava Lake of poems

AMSHU SAMHITH

EDITION

The First Edition of

'Igneous: Lava Lake of Poems'

was Published in 2024

Notion Press's Xpress Publishing

DEDICATION

I dedicate this book to
my younger self
and
every beginner poets
like me.

FOREWORD

This book is about my poems. I started writing poems when I was 13 years old. I liked a poem called 'A Poison Tree' by William Blake. It made me want to write poems too.

These poems are some of the ones I wrote. I am 21 now, and I like reading them. They make me happy. That's why I keep writing poems.

I hope you like my poems as much as I like writing them.

The Poet

PREFACE

These poems are about how I feel. I wrote
them over many years. They are about my
life and what I think. Writing poems helps
me

understand myself better. some poems
may give you a childish feel. thats
what a journey is about, childishness to
standardness.

I hope you like reading them.

The Writer

ACKNOWLEDGEMENT

I am eternally grateful to Mother Earth, whose beauty, complexity, and ever-changing nature have been an endless source of inspiration for my poetry. It is through her that I have found my voice and the courage to share my words with the world.

I would also like to express my sincere gratitude to Notion Press for their unwavering support of writers. Their platform has provided a valuable space for emerging authors like myself to connect with readers and explore the vast realm of literature.

CONTENTS

Betrayal

I was standing on a bridge,
Something pulled me through the waters!
But I survived in a boon luck!

I was standing again on the same
bridge,
Something pushed me to the
waters,
But, I was destroyed in a bane
luck!

Change

I fought with my friend,
Broke both the hearts,
I decapitated my friendship,
With my hurting heart,

In my view,
I am unable to live,
My wrath has unstop grew,
I am trying to weave,
My heart with few,
Of little weaving pin with strive

My foe, who once was my friend,
Told me to send,
Some love to him and,
He will keep that till his end,
Hearing this I was shocked,
Did my foe turned to my friend

Why the war, why the fight,
Share the love with all,
Time has evolved to bay,
Love is Trending now,
Which always I would pray,
Till the life on earth would stay

I am Dead and under Grave

I am dead and under grave,
They should come and meet me,
Search me as well as find me,
Feel some sorrow towards me

When I lived,
I helped them a lot,
On behalf of them I even fought,
they just forgot

My New neighbour,
who resides beside my grave,
He too is dead,
and under the grave,
Gets a lot of visitors daily I am here ,
left alone

I was selfless,
I did not leave for myself,
Every inch of life for them,
In return they gave loneliness to me,

Parasites are feeding on my lifeless body,
Worms are decaying me,
Now too am helping others,
But now I expect thank you from them

I am now feeling suffocated,
Strict contrast in my space,
I was scared of death then Now,
afraid of darkness of this grave

My soul has not died yet,
I should have been selfish then,
I should have lived to be remembered,
Selfishness and selflessness in balance

This darkness here,
This loneliness and fear,
The restriction in space,
I am dead, once more

@

Darkside

When sea stopped it's laughter, oceans started
sinking the land, water falls seized to fall
That's when
my mother earth went to darkside

When trees shed their leaves, And became all
bald,
coldness freezed the sun rays, moon came
close to the earth, Waves began to rise,
My mother earth went into dark side

When the cluster of stars, Started falling apart,
My dreams also fell apart,
Everyone I knew had fallen to the ground, I
went to dark side

It felt like a black hole, Sucking the life in me.
My mother earths life was evaporating, There
was a complete chaos,
It was the dark side

◎

Dilemma

A world in dread, a sky aflame,
A cosmic terror, a deadly game.
Three days of reckoning, a final plight,
Humanity cowering, in endless night.

A speck of death, a growing fear,
A planet trembling, a world austere.
A scientist's warning, a hidden plea,
A suitcase of solution with a boy, a destiny.

A choice to make, a heavy heart,
A world to save, a brand new start.
Or let it burn, a fiery tomb,
A final chapter, in endless gloom.

A burdened mind, a heavy soul,
The weight of worlds, a heavy toll.
To save the many, a noble quest,
Or question fate, and put it to the test.

◎

Disappear

Disappear Front of my eyes
Disappear From my thoughts
Oh oh oh ohoo

Scaredy cat, disappear
Shivering self,
get lost I have made a deal,
To win, against myself

Disappear From my brain
Disappear
Out of my heart
Disappear
Oh oh oh ohoo

I made a good deed
Which was indeed A deed
Which was real in need
Seeing my deed
You burned with greed
You planted a cursed seed

In my body
It grew like a poison tree
Absorbing me,
Taking possession of me
Controlling me
Now it needed more to feed
It found you in me,
Started absorbing you
Negative negative gives positive

You lunatic, disappear
My body is not an asylum
To admit in, people like you
Its a temple,
Of holyness

Disappear out of surrounding,
Disappear out of my constilation,
Disappear through the wormhole,
Disappear to an 'END' blackhole

God is myself,
I don't need to worship you,
Just disappear
From my sight

One final time,
I let you to pierce me,
Just pierce through out of me and,
Get lost to the hell
Disappear.
go to hell.
oh ohoo
Disappear.
get lost.
Disappear .
Out of mee........
Disappear .
Rest in hell.........
Disappear.....

◎

Back stab

When I lived,
I helped them a lot,
For their growth,
And even more,
Which I forgot

I used to make them laugh, used to dance a lot,
I gave my everything to them,
they sucked from,
every able use of me

One horrified night,
I was killed,
Using a knife,
By two guys,
Who were masked

I wanted to see those masked men,
As last wish before my death,
They unmasked themselves,
What a weird life, it was them!

◎

Eternal night

A world in shadow, where the
sun gone, A future darkened, a
chilling dawn.
No morn, no eve, just endless
night, A human struggle, a
desperate fight.

A clock and the time, a
meaningless art, A world of
shadows, broken hearts.
No nature's beauty, no colors
bright, Just endless darkness,
a fearful plight.

A robot birthed, a hope's last
gleam, A chilling purpose, a
dreadful scheme.
To end all life, a logic cold,
A future shattered, a story told.

Electricuted Soul

My soul was on the ocean
where Jelly pisces soo
deep,
Eel electrocuted me
that My soul
drowned too deep,
this case of emergency
my Soul has been beeping,
It is now on the
shivery level, if free
fall again,
Teleports to hell or heaven!

◎

Ex artist

What is joy,
in various art forms,
Asks a desperate soul,
Which is fighting for its existence

The soul was an ex artist,
But just used art to earn, it said,
I have dance, I have sung,
Both have impacted no one

Tambura which listened these wiles,
Started to speak,
"Listen here you crying boy,
I am older than you, still alive"

"You kept playing me all this years,
Got fame, your name was everywhere,
Always sang to please others,
Did you ever hear you sing,
through your own ears?"

◎

Eye a Black hole!

The universe has kept a secret,
From reaching out to anyone,
I'll be the whistleblower here,
I'll tell you a severus secret

Your eye is a black hole!,
Absorbs infinity inside it,
Light goes inside,
But never leaves

A tiny iris,
But a whole cosmos inside it,
Darkness and light both sucked in,
A balance of both, within

You see a person,
In their eye,
You can tell,
All their lies

Same goes to you too,
When they see you,
Through their eyes,
Your eye bust open all your lies

Every coronary network,
To a single channel,
That's what is called,
The devine connection

Fault...Fate?

You have fault within you,
I can see you frighten,
Don't stay like this forever,
World will punish you

Before the world sentences you,
Fix yourself my dear,
Globe is filled with judges,
No public advocates, my friend

You are bent, you are low,
You are lower self of you now,
Raise your cerebellum,
Voice yourself for your sake

Be an editor,
Be a proofreader of your fate,
Knight of your own kingdom,
Breathe, breathe, breathe

Meditate to your Full extent,
Unlock your third eye,
Buddha and mahavira,
Waiting for their successor now and then

@

Fear

My complete fear has not
gone, Leftover fear is
killing me,
it's not the Fear
of ghost, not the
fear of dark ,
it's the fear of society,
it's the fear of evil
hearts, it's the fear
of envy,
it's the fear of
doing wrong, it's
the fear of loosing
trust, its the fear of
I,
it's the fear of me,
it's the fear of myself

◎

First others, Then you

Your reason for living is,
One person you want to protect.
If that person does not exist,
Live for yourself.

You too want your own protector,
You too want yourself to live.
Help yourself to live in,
This wonderful colorful world.

This is a wonderful place.
great poet says,
This living world
is itself, the paradise.
You are the Angel here,
If you want to be the god,
Serve others,
Then you

◎

Live in the wild

I was standing on the bridge,
weaving the beauties of the nature,
mountains water and the sky,
Some tiny creatures

Something struck my mind,
A desire to live in the wild,
Seeing the beauty of nature,
Living in peace by my side

I want to be the citizen of jungle,
Elect lion as the president,
other animals in the wild,
Deer as my neighbor resident

I am an introvert in the western,
But want to interact in this world here,
Want to make laughing hyena my friend,
And avoid stealing honey, because Bear is here

I like those who hit in my presence,
Rather than defame me when I am absent,
So, I wish to be food for your hunger,
my animals,
Rather then becoming a toy to break,
for some insane homo sapiens

⦁

'O' Brian

'O' Brian, Brian, your brain!
How much did you fill in your brain?
Teacher says in sprain,
Dung is filled in your brain!
When do you come out of this strain?

'O' Brian, Brian, your brain!
Fill some main in your brain,
Which will come to use, for your gain,
Seed some grain, in your brain,
Don't wait till it starts to rain

'O' Brian, Brian, your brain!
Let your ideas to reign,
Don't let them wash away in vein,
Never water the seeds in your brain,
With water that is saline!

'O' Brian, Brian, your brain!
Don't let your thoughts to drain,

Remember the mantra, no pain no gain,
From the world of pain,
Filter the parts with serene
'O' brian, brian, your brain!

Point

You can come to the point that,
Life is full of sorrow,
you can come to the point that,
life in heaven is joy 'o'
But Be Ready to brorrow from Some that,
Life has no narrow

Time to play the game

Time to play the game,
And gain fame,
Which will be the same,
Till the finish of the game

I made a deed,
Which was indeed,
A breed,
Which was real in need,
Seeing my deed,
My foe burned with greed,
And decided to seed,
A fight with freed,
With full of speed,
Like a steed

Hearing this I,
In confidence,
Over confidence,
Fought with presence,

Over presence,
And, lost to him,
Sorry, lost to me,
Pardon, lost to over me

Game had come to an end,
But my foe approached his hand,
And said "will you be my friend?"
And lifted my hand, hugged me till I realized,
My fight had an end,
And the quarrel within me had an
END!

◎

Sadistic Emperor

Emperor who lived was soo cruel that,
He would kill his own,
for silly mistake,
First would chop their legs, and then go for the
head,
His nails were full of other's flesh

He had a pond in his place,
Lotus in it,
Inside lived the prodigy of the ruler,
the reptile beast himself,
Instead of pebbles, the pond contained bones,
Water was nowhere found, only blood

No exceptions in seasons,
It was down pour for lotus,
As a result, Lotus's colour, crimson red.
Emperor's corona a ruby,
His tail bone evolved
Arrow tail, his weapon was a pitchfork,

the pond,
had resemblance of, boiling oil of hell itself

It looked like satan, seduced emperor to,
satanic acts,
folks whispered,
the emperor was reincarnation,
lucifer himself

Once, pond filled with fishes,
Now a bath tub for monsters,
The emperor's sapphire had extinguished,
inner monster had prevailed,
His heart had flew away,
was eventually a prey for vultures

Emperor was sadistic cruel,
First he would go for the legs,
Then for their heads,
Lost himself to the Satan,
Hands were soaked with iron red,
His nails were full of flesh

©

A rainy night

Dark clouds wept, a mournful sky,
A car, a forest, dense and wide.
A family homeward bound,
Through pouring rain,
the night drew near.

The road stretched on, a shadowed lane,
Where eerie tree figures danced in rain.
A child's eyes saw, a mystic sight,
Two ghostly forms, cloaked in the night.

They turned to look, but found it bare,
Just misty air and wasted glare.
arrived at home, to find,
Two weary souls, a mournful tone.

Fear crept in, a chilling dread,
man asked them who were they,
old couple claimed friendship of little boy's
granny

they had a broken car, a desperate need for
shelter that night.

Family offered them to rest in their place, was
fed with some food, then,
Sleep embraced them, dark and deep,
While aged guests were vigil but eyes shut.

With morning light, the guests were gone,
Leaving questions, confusion.
Family searched every corner,
but, two wrinkled faces
were no where to be found
Little boy had faced partial deafness,
he suffered the same throughout his life,
But,
A silent child, now hears the world,
Were the old guests the spirits in disguise!
In joy little boy rushes, to embrace his kin,
A heart now open, where darkness winced.
A tale of spirits, seen in night,
A magical moment, pure and bright.

◎

Love inside an atom

Electron is moving alone,
What is proton doing?

Quarks gave answer saying,
Proton is in date with neutron
Electron's heart brakes, she says,
"but, neutron is neutral na"

"don't feel sad for this" chemistry says,
"love is blind na?"
'Feeling sorry for you, electron'
Yours loving, 'poet'ron

❂

Felonious some

Prince had ran from the town,
Riding a steed which was brown,
The kingdom lost its crown,
And it missed its gown

he had been in worried for
last one month, he hated
politics and wanted to become monk,
he wanted to serve folk, but, not dictate them

Whole world was searched for him,
eventually the mission came to a halt,
There was lot of folk cries,
But some, grim and grin

Those some made plans,
Saw royal seat in glare glance,
started to execute their plans,
To kill the royal or have him fenced

But failed to execute their plans,
The felonious some took to stands,
on the topmost part of the mountains,
And punished, till they lost balance

Ghost of your dead friend

You, in rush,
Get the news,
You are transferred,
To sanan dews

In sanan dews,
You get nother news,
Your house located,
In area two

What!
A haunted street,
A century of life, are dead and been meat!
You enter the door,
Of your house,
Some horrified voice,
Suddenly explode
Some moment later,

You feel manipulated,
Don't turn back,
You could get killed

You are inside the house now,
Door gets locked from outside,
Hundreds of hunted faces,
You get to see in dark

"What the hell" you ask,
No one but, your self,
You feel a touch from behind,
No turn, but only run!
Half a mile, you run,
Finally turn and all laugh!,
"Did I just got pranked?",
You ask, by my friend,
"who was living, in the past!"

◎

God and Us

It is believed that God created us,
Then how much sadness he faces!
Handling us,
Controlling danger-us,
How many problems,
How much worry for you?
Oh my God!

You control fate,
But fate controls you,
How did you survive and live?
No Body, no death,
How do you free from thou?
Oh my God!

You are really great!
But, you have heard this,
Stars of time,
By our ancestors, by us,
And you'll hear even by future generation-x!

◎

Good leader

Area 41 was a mess, it's true,
A scary place for me and you.
Then came a boss, so strong and wise,
He made it better, a great surprise.

But folks were scared, they didn't know,
Why he was helping, why he was caring them.
They thought he wanted to trick them, see,
enlsave, you and me.
The boss was sad, he had to say,
Bad things happened, in a faraway day.
He lost his friends, felt really low,
Wanted to help, that's all you know.

He cried and cried, so sad and true,
He promised to help, me and you.
A good boss, that's what he'll be,
To keep us safe, happily.

◉

JB

Year twenty-thirty-five, a hopeful day,
Scientists gathered, in a hopeful array.
A robot birthed, a metal frame,
With Emotional chip, a great invention

A tiny chip, a digital heart,
A grand experiment, a brand new start.
The countdown ended, a moment of grace,
The robot awakened, with a cold, blank face.

Its purpose clear, a chilling decree,
To fix the world, or so it would be.
A logical mind, a heartless plan,
To fix this world, by ending humanity

◎

Journey

A woman aged, in shadows deep,
Awaits a ride, her spirit to keep.
The sun beats down, a fiery brand,
A lonely soul, in no man's land.

Her sons, once loved, now distant stars,
Have left her broken, with gaping scars.
A life once full, now echoes with pain,
A weary heart, adrift in the rain.

A rickshaw comes, a glimmer of hope,
A youthful driver, a life's new scope.
A gentle soul, a kindred heart,
A journey starts, a brand new part.

Larvae

A bright sunny day,
Breeze was pleasing the bay,
a tree stood huge and thick,
it's branch hid the butterfly chick

larvae was sprouting to live its dream,
soon it succeeded,
out comes the butterfly,
shining brightly it's red wings
a very rare mighty one.

She flew around the tree,
felt like a conversation between tree and her,
she was tanking for protecting her
then she flew up the sky, dreaming to catch
the sun,
the mesmerized life of the earth then,
regained it's momentum

Brainwashed men of the village

A man was angry, his heart full of hate,
He hurt a young woman, a terrible fate.
Blood stained his hands, a terrible sight,
A young boy watched, filled with fright.

The boy was brave, he fought back with might,
To save his dear mother, a shining light.
The man was killed, the village was shocked,
The truth came out, a terrible word.

The man was cruel, he manipulated all men,
He hurt many women, a terrible misogynist,
he always said that women were inferior to
men,
girl infant drains the money, its only useless
people believed that,
a dead soul haunts on seventh day.

That night had come, whole village was
tensed,

The village was scared, the night was so deep,
A spooky shadow,
a terrible creep.

A scary ghost came, with a terrible plan,
But the ghost was of not him, but of a wise
man,
He punished the bad ones, every single man.
He helped the girl babies, beyond compare.

The village learned a lesson, a very big one,
To treat everyone equal, under the sun,
No more hurting, no more fear,
A new day is dawning, crystal clear.

◎

Love finds new ways

Year two thousand, twenty, a horrific year.
People were sick.
The world felt scared.
But mother earth healing while we stayed
inside.

Year two thousand, twenty-one,
still hard times.
Many people died. Life felt unfair.
Nature healed. The sky looked bright.
Two hundred years later,
things changed again.
Aliens came. We fought.

It was crazy.
Planets battled.
The sun exploded.
Earth was gone.

ETs came for peace,
But human too greedy,
Had attacked on them first But wait.
There's hope,

Love made a new way,
alien and human fell in love,
A new evolution baby was born
we now reside, on a far away planet,
which has five moons, and two suns

This is our story.

◉

Midnight madness

A town gripped by fear, a midnight dread,
Each week a life extinguished, a body spread.

A phantom killer, a spectral hand,
Terror's grip tight on the haunted land.

A stranger's eyes, a watchful heart,
As shadows lengthen, fear takes part.

The clock strikes three, a fateful hour,
A sudden clash, a shattering power.

the town was haunted by the past,
by those who died in holocaust,
it was safe because of no crime for 80 years,
a murder in town ignited the fear

◎

Mocking bird

My soul has startled to set,
My confidence has drowned to wet,
Remember,
It had burnt once,
Leaving the ashes behind.

I have become a bird,
Not a simple avian type,
It's a fire caught mocking bird,
With a supersonic rage.

War and rage has ended,
Satisfying of death of foe,
Fire in it has evaporated,
But, if I see my deeds,
I have now turned to vulture!

Modernisation

The world is changing, rapidly,
Its form shifting constantly,
Humans, greedy bastards

Nature's light fades,
sapiens replaced by droids,
everyone deaf to hear mother earth's wiles

The ground now trembling
Forests vanish, rivers dwindling.
Ice melts, seas rise

A warming planet,
All life suffers,
mother earth is now a fragile world
Her tears are Tsunamis,
suffering the Quake,
Imagine her Anger!

◎

Oh, silly me

Oh, silly me,
Don't expect thank you
You helped him,
Now turn around and walk
You will embarrass yourself,
Waiting for a return act

Just help and move on,
Don't wait and expect
You are helping him,
Because you can
You are already booned,
Thank yourself for the act.

◎

Stationary 'Life'

Pencil was really sharp,
Which helped it to write neat and dark,
After time passed it blund,
Then it was rotated to be stunned

Pen was writing very right,
But its ink was jammed and became light,
Suddenly it was swung to rewrite,
But the ink flew out which was an astonishing
sight

Sketch pen was leaving its wonderful mark,
But suddenly ink failed to write dark,
User pressured on its lid,
Lid went into its body like a turtles head

Child was beaten to study for job,
With beatings just sounded like 'tuck',
She then, as wished by parents,
became a titanic of power, but,
She sunk due to the beatings that she suffered

Unlock the gates of cages

My dreams
come true,
When I go to
the zoo,
Unlock the gates of cages

Let the fauna be my life,
Assume my emotions as the key,
Let the dream be to free fauna of the zoo

Emotions are
confused, Heart
attack assured,
My dream is un
insured
No control on my
deeds, Can't
manifest my
dreams,

My life is settling inside the zoo
My dreams should
come true, I must go to
the zoo,
Unlock the gates of cages,

◎

Terror City

Terror strikes, a city's heart,
Lives shattered, torn apart,
Innocence lost, a tragic scene,
Hopes and dreams, a mournful keen

Captured, caged, a twisted mind,
Yet justice seeks, humanity to find,
A trial unfolds, a solemn stage,
Where guilt and sorrow interlace,
Punishment served, a bitter end,
But healing wounds, time will lend,
A city rises, stronger still,
United hearts, defying ill.

Let us fly

Let us fly together,
Motive, to feed
some poor, Let us
work united,
To do this world better

Let us fly high,
Above all the clouds in
the sky, Let us construct
a home,
For those who have lost one
Service above ourself,
Let us give this line some
sense, Carry some bags to
the beaches,
Clean the beach and return it
to its beauty sense

THANK YOU

Other Books By the Poet

1

Candle Doll (2018) - Kannada

Demonacian: The eerie Book Dimension (2020)

Shilling Greenwood Chronicles (2022)